# HEART
# OF
# LIGHT

Lisa Levine is a Lightbeam of creative energy. In this varied collection of poetry, she reveals the depths of her perceptions while transporting us on a journey to engage with the people, places, and issues she holds dear. Lisa brings us into this present moment in which we are all grappling with very new and very old situations - disease, aging, death, family, memories, the natural world, travel, holiness, heartbreak, and perseverance. How do we move through this life? How do we find the courage to face our fears? As a Cantor, Rabbinic Pastor, and Chaplain, Reb Lisa reveals the wisdom of her experience and invites us to go within to find solace and insight through our innate spiritual awareness. Each poem asks us to stop, listen and receive the truth of what she has learned. The words are magical, flowing, and they ask us to reframe what we thought we already knew and what we take for granted. Lisa has encountered loss and adversity, yet she continues to soar and create beauty in the world. So can we! And her poems guide us on our way.

—Rabbi Hanna Tiferet Siegel

Lisa Levine's poetry is a rich tapestry of word images conveying the texture, depth and breadth of life and its complexities. This book leads you into an encounter with the essence of life and death, love and loss, hope and despair. And in the final analysis, a spirit of hope prevails.

—Dr. Reb Simcha Paull Raphael founder of the DAAT
Institute and author of *Jewish Views of the Afterlife*

The prayers in this volume are honest and real in their eloquent simplicity. They speak directly to the heart, to the fullness of the human condition and to our most basic yearning for meaning. There is great redemptive power in the beauty of the visual arts and the power of poetic expression. Dive in and then linger a while.

—Rabbi Karyn Kedar author of *Amen: Seeking Presence with
Prayer, Poetry, and Mindfulness Practice*

Lisa Levine dedicates her poetry collection, *Heart of Light*, "To everyone who has suffered loss." It is with that devotion—and in that spirit—that these messages from her own heart unfold. She shares the intimacy of loss with her reader and offers solace through her prayerful, earth-based, mystical Jewish perspective. In "Aliyah," she shares her blessing for all of us: "Shalom, Salaam, Peace. Going up, way up."

—Rachel Kann, author of *How to Bless the New Moon*,
(WORD: Bruce Geller Memorial Prize)

Each section of *Heart of Light* brims with thoughtful and rich poetry. Reb Lisa's imagery is both familiar and new at the same time, allowing readers to find meaning in every line. You will not regret luxuriating in her text.

—Stacey Zisook Robinson, poet and essayist, author of
*Dancing in the Palm of God's Hand* and *A Remembrance of Blue*

# HEART OF LIGHT

POEMS OF LONGING, LOSS, & LIFE

## LISA LEVINE
ARTWORK BY JULIE SILVER

Copyright © 2020 by Lisa Levine
Heart of Light Press
Brookeville, Maryland

All rights reserved. No part of this book may be reproduced, stored in a retrieval system or transmitted by any means, electronic, mechanical photocopying, recording or otherwise, without written permission of the author.

ISBN: 978-0-578-70488-3

Art by Julie Silver © 2016-2020
www.juliesilver.com

"In The Blink of an Eye," "Freedom" and "Dreams" first appeared in *Yoga Shalom* published in 2011 by URJ Press.

To everyone who has suffered loss,
may hope abide.

## Table of Contents

**INTRODUCTION** ............................................................. i

**HEART SPIRITS** ............................................................ 1

    In The Blink of an Eye ............................................. 3

    The Linden Tree ...................................................... 4

    For Mary ................................................................. 6

    Passover Table ........................................................ 9

    Reincarnation ........................................................ 10

    Butterfly ................................................................ 13

    A River Called Heaven ........................................... 14

    Into Dark Places ................................................... 16

    Unraveling ............................................................ 18

    Dreams ................................................................. 21

    In Memoriam ....................................................... 23

    Good Ending ........................................................ 24

**HEART JOURNEYS** ...................................................... 27

    Coming Home ...................................................... 28

    The Train North ................................................... 30

    Aliyah .................................................................. 32

    Wailing Wall ........................................................ 34

    Shabbat Walk ...................................................... 36

    S'fat ..................................................................... 38

    Kibbutz Enat ........................................................ 40

    Tel Aviv ............................................................... 42

| | |
|---|---|
| Table for One | 45 |
| Pollination | 46 |
| Cuba Triumphara! | 48 |
| Kaleidoscope | 50 |

**HEART BLESSINGS** ........................................................... 53

| | |
|---|---|
| I Came to Believe | 54 |
| Where I'm From | 59 |
| Aloneness | 61 |
| Let It Flow | 62 |
| Dirt Manicure | 64 |
| Letting Go | 67 |
| The Wall | 68 |
| The Rainbow | 71 |
| My Mask | 72 |
| Powerless | 74 |
| Don't Sweat the Small Stuff | 76 |
| Aging Gracefully | 78 |
| For Emily | 80 |
| Tidal Pool | 83 |
| Sparks | 84 |
| Returning to the Table, a **Midrash** poem | 86 |
| Freedom | 89 |
| The Light of You | 90 |

# INTRODUCTION

My relationship with words began when I learned to play guitar and sing at the age of eight. From a very young age, I memorized hundreds of songs to perform at home, school, and later at coffee houses and other venues. Learning the music of the artists of the 60s and 70s, including the late great Debbie Friedman, eventually inspired me to write my own prose and music.

Born and raised in Bakersfield CA, I went to Jewish summer camp and traveled to Israel the summer of my 16th year and lived on Kibbutz Enat. That is where my love affair with Israel began and poetry took a major role in capturing my experience. I attended the University of California Irvine on a vocal scholarship and earned my Bachelor of Arts degree in music, returning to Israel for my junior year abroad. Again, poetry and writing were my companions. After undergraduate school I was called to the vocation of Cantor and was accepted into a graduate seminary in New York. I sold everything and moved across the country to attend Hebrew Union College-Jewish

Institute of Religion School of Sacred Music. It was an intense challenge and it was made easier because of words. Words calmed and nurtured me, focused and challenged me to create. I practiced self-care through writing, yoga, and music.

After ordination and during the three decades of service as a Cantor which followed, I deepened my connection to music and writing. My healing songs, *"Ruach Elohim"* and *"MiSheberach"* flowed from me like water. A catalogue of more than 150 prayers and songs followed. When I wrote my prayer embodiment book *Yoga Shalom*, I decided to include poems and kavannot (creative prayers) with each chapter. It felt good to express my feelings and frustrations with the world around me.

The deaths of my older brother and mother in a one year period threw me into an emotional tailspin as sadness and grief engulfed me. It was amplified by the fact that I had to continue to perform my duties as Cantor, which included funerals as well as life cycle events filled with joy. I stuffed my feelings deep inside me, slapped a smile on my face, and kept on going. Four months after my mother's death, my sister Sharon died of a drug overdose. These indelible losses dramatically changed the trajectory of my life.

The absence of time to grieve while trying to make sense of life, motivated my entrance into the Aleph Rabbinic Pastors Program, which, in turn, led to the study of

Clinical Pastoral Education. This intense self-examination helped me process and understand what ALL faith traditions teach about grief and death. In my own journey, finally giving myself time to properly grieve, I was able to help others deal with their end of life issues and begin my healing from the devastating losses I had suffered. During this time of self-reflection, I began pouring my grief, longing, pain, and gratitude into the writing of poetry. This collection is the result. It has given me a window for optimism and hope.

Last December at the URJ Biennial in Chicago, I reunited with my friend Julie Silver. Already a celebrated songwriter and wordsmith herself, Julie had found a new passion as a visual artist. I connected deeply with her art and felt that it expressed the same longing, loss, and love as my poems. An idea began to form about our collaboration in this book. Julie's beautiful images add depth of meaning to this collection. For the blessing of Julie's talent and friendship I am truly grateful.

I wish to thank my editor, Ellen Collins, for her patient direction and honesty in helping me cull these 41 poems from the hundreds I gave her. Thank you to Crystal Heidel for designing the book, and to George Beckerman and Mary Helms (of blessed memory) for making the connection among us. Thank you to Dr. Simcha Raphael for his teachings and guidance through the world of Jewish grief and the afterlife. Thank you to Rabbi Hanna Tiferet Siegel

and all of my teachers and mentors in the Aleph Rabbinic Pastors Program. Thank you to my clinical pastoral supervisors: Geofrey Tio of Community Care Chaplains, Don Clem & Beth Godfrey of Medstar Georgetown University Hospital, as well as the CPE cohorts, patients, family and friends who inspired the words on these pages. I want to thank my family and friends in Israel for always making me feel so loved and my Cuban friends for showing me the strength which is needed to carry on. Thank you to my family for your unwavering love and support through all of the ups and downs, losses and moves we have weathered together.

Life continues to have its devastations. In the age of Coronavirus, the realities of death and life, as well as gratitude for what we have, mean more than ever before. I continue to celebrate the good, the bad, and the ugly. I invite you to delve into the words which follow. My prayer is that you will use these poems for worship, prayer, meditation and healing, as we journey through this world of tragedy and joy together.

# HEART SPIRITS

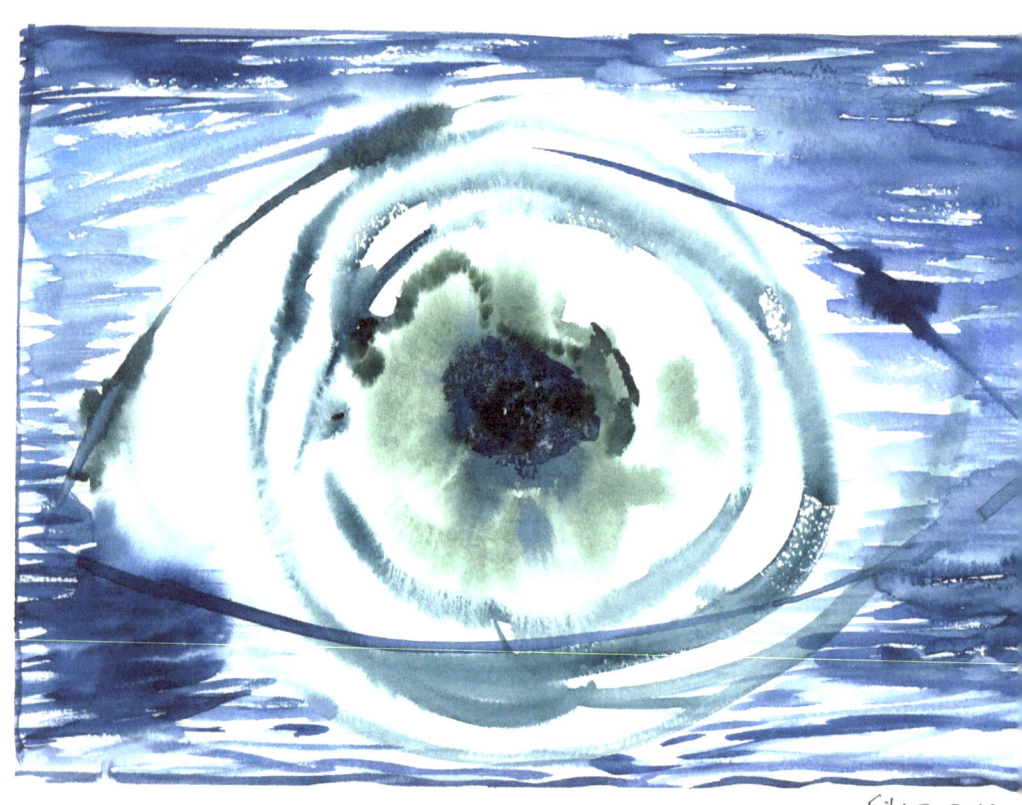

**In The Blink of an Eye**

In the blink of an eye
the whole world changes
people that we love
suddenly are gone.
All that we have
is but lent to us
in the blink of an eye
ashes turn to dust.

In the blink of an eye
our lives flash before us
thinking of things
that we should have done.
Promises made
promises broken,
in the blink of an eye
we feel so alone.

We turn to the One
from whom we draw comfort
when family and friends
aren't enough.
We look for the strength
from deep inside us
the spirit of our loved one
forever in our hearts.

 | LISA LEVINE

**The Linden Tree**

The linden tree is starting to bloom.
It dies off each year
and loses its leaves,
baring the lonely branches
to the cold winter and yet
with the first sign of spring
gives me a little temptation.
It pops again and is reborn.
Soon it will be covered
with full green, lush foliage,
providing shade and shelter,
home to the lost.

So, too, that spirit
which has left its body,
escaping the earth and leaving behind,
pained and hurting, the living, the lonely
bereft and lost
my soul branches are bare and raw to the cold,
my heart is laid open to the ravages of darkness
and yet.....

When a light of memory
shines in to warm that grieving,
a flame is reborn,
the leaves of love
are the foliage,
the lush remembrances of words,
the warm feeling of embraces.
Sheltered and shaded
I am certain
that everything returns
to its Source.

Tree and branch
wind and leaf
fir and frond
arms and eyes and lips and hearts.
Soul memory
intertwined with my branches.
Love is never lost.

**For Mary**

Dying
takes a lot of strength,
especially when you can't move,
when all you do is listen
deeply
and feel everything
inside.
It all hurts.

I see this incredible effort,
as you lift your arm,
and as you weep
when you hear my voice
praying for you.
I see the love
in your beautiful eyes.

You lift me and send me up
toward the clouds.
God is close.

I pray for you,
for strength to leave
this earthly space,
for you to enter
the heaven of poetry
and beautiful words
and love,
and in the pools
of your deep blues
your soul is revealed.

I dive in.
Enveloped in your truth.
I wish I could take your pain.

It takes a lot of strength
to die.

**Passover Table**

Sorting through the silver,
I picture my grandmother's hands
as mine.
Preparing for the holiday
with tempered measure,
spoon by spoon,
fork by fork,
each in its rightful place
ready to be engaged
in the promise of food
plentiful and rich.

Stark contrast to her *shtetl* home
always scratching for a bite,
this country paved with gold
gave off its bounty
to our family,
a sacred
gathering place,
cleaning, placing, watching,
protecting all
she had built,
and preserving it all
for me
so that I could be
sorting the silver
today.

**Reincarnation**

Death is not a door.
Closing at the end of life
rather, death
is a window,
opening wide
into a dimension and place
where souls are free to travel
unadorned and unencumbered.
Each recitation of the mourners *Kaddish*
ushers the *neshama*, soul, to a place
of sacred eternal rest,
soaring higher and higher and higher
with each utterance of the holy words.

After one year that soul
finally breaks free
of its earthly trappings
and becomes one with *Ein Sof*,
the unseen Source,
ready to redeploy
to its next iteration
of life.

HEART OF LIGHT |

**Butterfly**

Yesterday I saw a butterfly.
It hovered before my weepy eyes
And whispered to me.

*Please don't mourn and cry*
*because my love will never die.*
*My light is one*
*that will never be extinguished,*
*and although my body has gone,*
*my spirit and memory will live on*
*through your light and music and love.*
*My soul will soar on and on and on*
*beyond the confines of this world,*
*unconstrained by earthly woes.*
*I'm free now let me go.*

Yesterday I saw a butterfly
perfect in its symmetry and color,
its wings gracefully navigating the wind,
and I knew
you would always be with me.

 | LISA LEVINE

**A River Called Heaven**

There's a river called heaven,
where Dad's soul has gone to be,
where the fish are always biting,
and the brandy's always free,
It's there you'll find him drifting,
smiling and at peace,
on that river called heaven,
fishing for eternity.

Golfing, camping, fishing, boating—
we were raised on all of these,
but the steelhead runs at Klamath
are my fondest memories.
And through it all he worked like crazy,
so we'd have the things we'd need,
he was the strongest man I've ever known,
his strength is inside me.

Yes, there's a river called heaven,
Marvin's spirit's surely there,
in his fishing hat and slicker,
and his worn-out captain's chair.
And someday we'll be there with him,
to land the biggest one by far,
and together we will smoke it,
and put it into pint-sized jars.

But 'til then, Dad, Marv, old buddy,
we know you are at peace.
On that river called heaven,
fish are biting constantly,
the river that's called heaven,
fishing for eternity.

 | LISA LEVINE

### Into Dark Places

Fractionated light shines through the clouds
casting a glimmer over the rain-drenched trees,
red and orange, yellow and brown.
As the season turns from light to darkness
the warmth of the sun's rays
penetrates the eerie sky,
bring a sense of hope
and peace to my heart.

This moment opens a window—
so many memories of love and friendship
so many moments of strife and disappointment.
Through the devastation of life,
people who shine like sun beams
bring me back to what really matters
like the leaves falling from the trees
and the rain falling from the sky,
part of the regeneration of life.
So too
continuous goodbyes
in order for rebirth
to happen,
and though it's painful
and there is much grief involved,
there is also much promise.

That seed of knowing
was planted in death
and the grief suffered
has grown into a strong sapling
ready to become a mighty oak.

And so our lives
are a series of growths
from strength to strength,
from death to life,
from hellos and goodbyes,
from laughter and tears
from mourning to dancing
from triumphs and disappointments
to deep learning,
deep gratitude,
Eternal love,
unfathomable intentional being.

### Unraveling

You spent the last few months
unraveling a ball of yarn
with great patience and devotion
as though it was
the most important thing
in the world.
I was always amazed
at your fortitude in that,
never fazed, never frustrated,
just like your life.
A pioneer and working wife
before that was even a thing,
creating
so many beautiful knits,
crafting and blocking,
wearing them all
with grace and beauty.

That's how you lived,
with humor and strength,
Your come-backs were always quick,
Wit was easy for you.
In your quiet and devoted way
you never asked much
yet we always gave all.
The presence you brought

after your sudden departure
feels like a dark deep hole
that can't be filled
except with the love we have,
the memories we share,
and the blessings of family.
Those who loved you are here.
Bidding you a final farewell.
Your yarn finally free from knots,
Your final sweater blocked.
Ready to wear.

**Dreams**

There are people
we meet in our dreams
deep pools of memory.
A voice, a gesture, a movement
the color of an eye
sparkling true
an accent
speaking in a way that is familiar.
We see hands grasping ours
drawing us into the past.
There
just beyond our worldly vision
a spirit standing next to us
we speak
expecting to hear an answer
to a questions we've always asked.
What's for dinner?
Can I have that recipe?
Did my package arrive?
Those who have moved on
are in our heads all the time
speaking through us
whispering the answers
to all our hidden questions
sometimes knowing us better
than we know
ourselves.

**In Memoriam**

There isn't a day that goes by
that I don't think of you,
my lifetime teacher.
You are always in my mind
even though we are apart.
The wonderful times
we shared together,
are a prayer in my heart.

Flower and tree, river and sky,
always a story to share.
A loving adventurous life
has been God's gift to you.
Thank you for sharing part of it
with me, your lifetime student.

My spirit is with you now,
and my way of being there
to see you off.
Now you are traveling free
over the water and back to the earth
you so lovingly shared with me.

**Good Ending**

When it's my time,
let me go and wish me well.
Turn down the lights and sing me away,
shepherd my spirit to a place of light,
open a window
so I can fly.

Life is so fragile,
like a fading rose.
Let me fade
as nature meant me to.
Free to join the flow
of the river.

# HEART JOURNEYS

**Coming Home**

I grab my bag and follow the
stream of Jews with black hats
the faithful
the seekers
to the port of entry
wigs and boots, tank shirts.
shorts and long skirts.
All shapes, sizes
colors
lines stretched out like fences
adorned with vines of
multicolored flowers
moving slowly toward the land
the promise.
Dancing through to the other side
what greets me is the biggest hall
of luggage on the planet
where to start?
Information of course,
*Lama lo?* why not?
Modern and bi-lingual.

HEART OF LIGHT |

Time is suspended, motionless.
My eyes soak up the scene.
A lovely stranger helps
buy a train ticket
guides me to the platform
so kind.
Hebrew, English, Arabic, Spanish
washing over me
like a gentle wave
a vindaloo of culture
horns and train engines
familiar and foreign.
Coming home.

### The Train North

Twin boys playing games on their phones
one with a thumb in his mouth,
one with a water bottle
their Hebrew easier to understand
than the rapid chatter of the excited teens
when the soldier asks them to quiet down
they just laugh, then whisper. Loudly!
The overweight housewife works
a crossword puzzle while
the big bearded guy next to her
watches a movie on his phone.
Then there is the lithe young man
dressed all in black
with his JVC headphones
he seems to be choreographing a dance
as his hands move to the music in his ears.
I imagine the sound.
We sway and clatter over the rails
the sea to our left along the coast
toward the hills of *Ein Hod*.

They all make up this train community

The exotic lady
her colorful turban tower
defining her religious ways
suddenly notices a big black man and asks,
"Where are you from?"
He says "the Ivory Coast"
She responds thoughtfully,
"You are an amazing man,
I can tell by looking at you-
You are what a person should be"
How does she know that?
Is she peering into his soul?
Or is she enamored by his presence?
Am I what a person should be?
What does she see
when she looks at me?

### Aliyah

They call it going up
not only because Jerusalem
is built on hilltops
but because as I ascend
I feel my spirit rising too.
It is déjà vu,
like I know the way.

The spirits of my ancestors,
the angels of peace,
are guiding me,
and the angels of war
are chanting:
"Peace to this land,
shalom to this holy city."

I am on bus 904,
and notice the signs
in Arabic and Hebrew,
just like the USA
in English and Spanish.
Living side by side
with our Palestinian neighbors.

Going up.

It means rising above,
connecting with the higher,
One God,
Abraham Muhammed Jesus,
connected and diverse.
Messengers of the Word,
purveyors of peace.

Shalom, Salaam, Peace.

Going up,
way up.

### Wailing Wall

My hands are touching the Wall.
Feeling the vibrations,
seeking a crevice
to place my prayers,
my hopes and dreams
for our people
so long in struggle.
The wall is jagged
and smooth
at the same time,
telling, showing
war and peace and war.
The faithful flock here
to be heard.
They cry out
the sound is almost
too much to bear.

Sacred pilgrimage,
spirit reborn,
praying, whispering,
crying, swaying
I back away slowly
not turning my face
or my spirit
from this place.

And when standing in front
of the open ark,
I will picture my prayer note
and this wall, wailing
reminding me
of the sacred
Eternal promise
of peace.

 | LISA LEVINE

**Shabbat Walk**

There is something beautiful
and poetic
about the city of Jerusalem
with all of her golden stone,
her tree-lined neighborhoods,
flowers overflowing from patios.

There is something beautiful
and peaceful
about Shabbat in the City of Gold,
families walking together
hand in hand, slowly relishing
the color of the sky
and the day of rest to come.

There is something beautiful
and holy
about the way the sun
shines and reflects
off the ancient hills
telling tales of layers
and centuries of war.

There is something beautiful
about the tall cypress trees
retelling the story of peace,
refusing to fall
like the people whose roots
are deep and connected.

There is something beautiful,
unforgettably, indelibly, and eternally
etched upon my heart.
It is a love unlike any other,
worth defending and dying for,
a love grounded in the faithful,
unconditional and unwavering.

There is something beautiful
about this holy place,
eternal, complicated, peaceful,
prone to argument, loud,
unforgiving and forgiven,
like the gift of knowledge
that
just
is.

### S'fat

Winding roadway up
hairpin mystery,
ancient pathway
to the mystical city
at the top of the mountain,
Imagining a donkey
struggling
or a woman
with a water jug balanced
on her head,
a most challenging climb
to wash and feed,
live or die,
uneven stones
worn smooth from wear,
the birthplace
of the Sabbath Bride,
incubator
for the *Sefirot*,
energy centers
mystical awakenings,
Tree of Life.

Pulsating pathways
of art and prayer
heart opening,
spirit opening,
carrying me
like the jug
into alignment with
all the courageous women
whose steps trod this path
feeling
their journey.
Hearing their prayers,
thousands of words,
swirls of spirits
above and around me,
through the windows and doorways,
eerily whispering
*welcome, welcome.*

 | LISA LEVINE

### Kibbutz Enat

This place of rebirth and history
indelibly etched in me
since a summer adventure at sixteen,
weeding cotton and washing dishes.

That was where my love affair began,
a lifelong obsession with the land and her people.

Our volunteer hut on the edges of the cotton fields
filled with music and flying cockroaches,
the village of *Rosh Haayin* and the ruins
where we hiked to smoke,
soul awakening
bearing fruit I'm still savouring.

Here, the lifelong friendships,
still family, so precious,
returning decades later
and time stands still.
Masha is in her kitchen,
creating tasty cakes,
Aviram serving sweet Turkish coffee,
relaxing in the garden,
a hot day under the shade,
laughing and noshing,
drinking and reminiscing
about those we've lost,
ghosts in a dream
preserved like a perfect lemon
in sweetness and tears.

HEART OF LIGHT |

## Tel Aviv

It's really been quite fantastic,
spending these few luxurious weeks
traveling in *Eretz Yisrael*.
From the cool evening breezes
off the sea
to the pulsating beat
of the Carmel Street market,
to Independence Park,
Dizengoff fashions,
and cafés filled with life.

This magical place,
so advanced and yet
so backwards sometimes,
unpredictable and yet
so safe.
Feeling like everything and everyone
has my back.

In this city
there's a complete sense
of calm, of peace,
like the vortex of a huge storm.
I am in the eye
of *namaste*,
renewed and energized
by the sheer beauty
of it all.

 | LISA LEVINE

**Table for One**

Eating alone
is never my preference,
but sometimes
in a far-away place,
wandering into an exotic
local hot spot,
it feels so decadent
not to have to speak
except to order,
no one to enjoy
except myself.
A glass of vino,
delectable freshness of
falafel fusion,
a complete experience
in mindful eating.
Noticing everything—
couples,
groups,
families,
chatting and enjoying
under the subdued lighting.
Quiet elegance.
My heart accepts it.
Feeling the love,
me, myself, and I.

 | LISA LEVINE

## Pollination

The buzz of Tel Aviv,
a vibrant, pulsing energy,
sand and sea, sky and wind,
the beat of a people
free and open
yet keenly aware
of every freedom.
One moment away
from nothing and everything,
complicated and easy,
an intersection of cultures and languages,
styles and peculiarities,
lights and bikinis,
skateboards and T-shirts,
well-guarded and girded
against violence,
a protected airspace.

And yet the pulse feels
so free and easy and beautiful
like the whole world revolves
right around all of it,
colorful and rare,
a jewel of the Mediterranean.

# HEART OF LIGHT

*Show me your heart*
*Hold me in your beat*
*Caress me in your life*
*Expose me to your secrets*
*Unfold me to your truths.*

The vibration
like bees
buzzing around the flowers.

I drink.

 | LISA LEVINE

**Cuba Triumphara!**

I am awakened at 5:00 this morning
by the sound of shouting voices.
A pair of camel buses,
in their behemoth form
unload children onto the street.
They look up and wave to me,
as if this is a normal day,
busloads of school children
on a mission with walking feet.

There is a fire deep inside them,
they burn for social justice,
marching in the Havana streets,
hundreds of thousands strong
at the call of their hero.
All else is forgotten.
They are herded
by their shepherd
and equality for all.

It is a gift,
this chance to witness history.
The reality of Cuba
is so different than we thought.
With the fire deep inside them
they burn for social justice,
for the sake of their people's honor
they answer Fidel's call.

They chant
"Long live Fidel Castro!
Utopia for all!
We march for social justice!
*Cuba triumphara!*"

 | LISA LEVINE

## Kaleidoscope

Blue on blue, red on red, green on green.
Vibrant hues reflecting this rainbow-drenched country,
a kaleidoscope of colors extending to the horizon,
the magical intersection of slavery and freedom,
of religion and tribalism, a cultural woven tapestry
reaching back through the centuries,
bringing the spirit
of the Cuban people and culture to life.
Poor and yet happy, they shoulder on
despite the many challenges and complications
that plague their lives.

Fidel, the Moses of the Cuban people,
freed them from tyranny and brought them to
    redemption—a dream lost.
Through their struggle, the Jews of Cuba
continue to thrive.
Their love for Israel and our history and Torah
are the cornerstones of their lives.
The perseverance and strength
of their determination to survive,
like all of our ancestors wherever they have lived,
are awe-inspiring and compelling,
and the world they embrace.
Worthy of the world to come!

My heart is with you, *mi corason*,
my Jews of Cuba.
I will not abandon you nor will I ever forget
your kindnesses and your friendships.
You are with me always.

*Am Yisrael Chai and Viva Cuba!*

# HEART BLESSINGS

**I Came to Believe**

I came to believe,
after burying my brother,
that life is fleeting and cruel,
and that what we do for others
matters.

I came to believe,
after burying my mother,
that dying of a broken heart
is not only possible,
it happens.

I came to believe,
after burying my sister,
that I couldn't save her
and I can't save the world,
nor do I want to.

I came to believe,
after losing my job,
that sexual harassment is common,
that doing the right thing
usually ends badly.

I came to believe
that people with money
are in control,
and they use that control
to get what they want.

I came to believe,
after a short separation,
that freedom doesn't always
bring happiness,
and love comes with imperfections.

I came to believe,
after my children grew up
and left to strike out on their own,
they would always need me
no matter how old they are.
I was right.

I came to believe
that having time to do
what means most to me,
means that I don't have to do
what others want me to do.

I came to believe
that getting older
means listening better,
and that talking
usually doesn't mean as much.

I came to believe
that love is something
we invest time in,
and that ignoring the ones we love
doesn't help us feel better.

I came to believe
things must be tidied up,
stuff is expendable,
people are not.

I came to believe
that whatever it is I want to do
I need to do now,
because time is my vehicle
and it will crash.

That all I am is these words
and someday
they are all
that will be left
of
me.

HEART OF LIGHT |

## Where I'm From
after George Ella Wheeler

I'm from the almond and orange trees of California,
where the scent of blossoms was always strong.
I'm from the hard working immigrants of the shtetl
who settled near San Joaquin Valley farms.
I'm from a Jewish family where food was always fine.
I'm from the pawn shop counter
where I wrapped gifts when I was nine.
I'm from hand-me-downs and Birkenstocks,
from stage and choral risers.
used guitars and rhymes,
I'm from pain and joy and slavery,
from dancing and yoga and song,
from the freedom to pray and celebrate
in religious throng.
I'm from love and hate and unity
with trees and plants and seeds.
I'm from the Klamath River
and giant redwood trees.
I'm from everything holy
and some things not so great,
but with all my breath and being
I will always celebrate
where I'm from.

**Aloneness**

Can the hole
which is my heart
be filled with silence
and in that silence
perhaps,
perhaps,
I'll be able
to listen
and
finally
hear?

**Let It Flow**

Music flows from a well
inside me.
directed by a Higher power,
inspired
from a deeper place.

Anger, joy,
grief and memory
love and hate
give me the spark
to create.

Music flows from a well
deep inside me
the Source, *Shefa*
gushing
emotions
into the world.

Dancing
from reality
into mindfulness
focused
for healing.

Music flows from a well
inside me,
My spine fills
with spirit renewing
waters.

 | LISA LEVINE

**Dirt Manicure**

Today I gave myself
a dirt manicure,
the first this spring.
It felt decadent, digging
in the soil, rubbing
up against the worms, watching
them squiggle away from my trowel,
slither down into the loamy darkness.

Me, attacking the weeds,
mounding them up,
and tossing them away
like so many pains of life
no longer needed.
Just the dirt feeling so real,
bringing up the gratitude of imperfection,
the work of my hands
so bone wearily satisfying
and so beautifully heartfelt.

Flowers in 3-D,
vibrant and fragrant, bee-filled.
Buzzing sounds of rebirth,
pollination and procreation,
new life and new possibilities.
Deep cleaning of my spirit.

Smiling
from a place I want to know
more often,
I look down
and see the dirt under my nails,
the best manicure
ever.

**Letting Go**

I have a dream
of living my life
out of the world's grasp,
floating along in the cool breeze,
my feet barely touching
the sand.
Forgetting the social worlds,
the projects, promotions,
just reading
and walking the beach
and writing
soaking up the rays,
alive in the air, close
to forest and sea
in a quiet, humble
space.
Free.

### The Wall

Your wall
It pushes back
on every word
is it a wall against me
or is it a wall against the world?
My wall goes up
when I feel your wall
Why do we do it?
build this wall
between us
this emotional,
concrete edifice.
Let's dissolve it
and let our hearts meet
our minds connect
our thoughts intermingle
lets find an understanding
instead of putting up this
wall of words.
just get rid of the wall
tear it down
exist as we are.

No egos.
No defenses.
No anger.
No judgements.
No expectations.
No emails.
No texts.
Just eyes,
Ears,
Hearts,
Hands,
The wall,
poof.
Gone.

**The Rainbow**

Today there was the most beautiful
rainbow above me,
yellow and purple and red, blue and green,
as though God had messaged me.

*Join hands for justice...*
*join hands for peace,*
*join hands for a time*
*when hatred will cease.*

The colors of the rainbow
reminded me that
everyone is a rainbow.
I am a rainbow.
      My heart is a rainbow.
           My spirit is a rainbow.

In that moment imagining—
more diversity,
more change,
more growth.
In that moment believing,
channeling my heart
toward the message of the rainbow,
    *send a prayer of healing through our land.*

That means everyone.
That means me.

 | LISA LEVINE

**My Mask**

My mask
my way
of keeping others at arm's length,
where the safety of my joy
cannot be touched.
My hurts and traumas
are tucked away
in a safe compartment.
Hidden under my mask of smiles,
so you don't see my pain.
I see you.
Your eyes expose
what your mouth keeps hidden.

Lift the mask,
smile with your heart,
give us both a way
to know,
how to begin
to love again.

HEART OF LIGHT |

 | LISA LEVINE

**Powerless**

The T.V. is on and selling
whatever it is we must have—
a necklace, a bag, a bowl, a dress.
Like the regurgitation of too much food

Trying to wrap my head around
this country of so much plenty
when so many are in need,
so many everywhere but especially
my friends in *Namatumba, Uganda,*
going hungry.
They could and would greedily feed
an entire family on what we throw away.
Just one handbag
would sustain them for a week,
all the food wasted
could be for them.
Stepping into the shower
feeling abundant hot water
reminds me of my friends there
with no running water.
They walk for hours just to bring
a jug to drink or to bathe.
I feel guilt ridden and angry,
for those who do not have.

Something inside longs to fix that,
to stop the waste
and the greed.
How much does one person need
to feel happy?

 | LISA LEVINE

**Don't Sweat the Small Stuff**

When put into perspective
it becomes easier to forgive
and move past the small stuff
like tracking in mud
or leaving the toilet seat up.

With the bigger stuff,
words that can't be taken back
yelling and blaming
looping in my head,
it's a lot harder.

Then something happens
like COVID-19
or a mass shooting
and just like that
it snaps me back
to love.

Perspective.
It makes all the difference.

**Aging Gracefully**

I have felt beautiful my whole life.
I guess it's from my mother telling me so.
The first boy who kissed me,
said I was lovely, and he must have known.
When I fell in Jerusalem and cut my forehead,
the nurse speaking Hebrew said, "*hi nora yafah.*"
I knew that meant "she is quite beautiful,"
and even though I was in pain bleeding, I smiled.
My husband tells me every day,
and my daughter too,
and here I am moving into old age
feeling not that way at all.
Every crack and line and indentation,
every sag in my neck and bulge in my body
comes laughing at me from the mirror.
All that's happened in my life is now
piled on me like a layer of caking mud,
all of the injustices, indulgences and sorrows,
the grief and the disappointments
obscuring the person I am.
It may be time to peel back and reveal
the new version of the old version of me.
On the inside, slightly worn
On the outside, wisdom earned
inside out.
An exchange of beauty.

Age will do that I suppose, something
I'm trying to avoid.
Seeing the younger, beautiful women,
I think, "someday you'll know."

It's what's on the inside that keeps you sane
when everything on the outside
goes.

fish face

 | LISA LEVINE

**For Emily**

Forever and ever,
that's the way it is.
Unchanging,
unfettered,
nothing to be said.
Just the waves,
sun and the sand,
just us two
the way we've always been.

Forever and ever
as it's meant to be,
enjoying only the present
not what might have been.
Here we are together
as just from the start,
my daughter,
my beauty,
embedded in my heart.

And when all that's left is
silent memory,
I hope you'll return here
and feel calm and free.
Feel my spirit linger,
the love we'll always share,
my body may be gone
but our laughter
is always there.

Forever and ever
the way we've always been
just you and me
together
voice and violin.
We are never parted,
feelings do not die.
Tears will wash the pain
from your heart.

 | LISA LEVINE

SKI

## Tidal Pool

Everything returns
back to the Source,
the challenges of life
swept away with the tide.
Survival is connected
with the flow of the waters,
regenerated and renewed
with each breath in silence.

We strive and we work
until we are loved,
and yet within ourselves
lies the true Source of strength.
The ebb and flow,
the constant world of change,
is what motivates our struggle
to find our way through the pain.

Under the surface,
bubbling possibility,
every-changing,
ever-beckoning.
Embrace the flow
discover the light of truth
the deepest pool
of self-knowing.

**Sparks**

Sparks of flame
        illuminating dark places,
                bringing promise
                        to a broken heart,
to a broken world.

Sparks of light
        shining into a crevasse,
                seemingly bottomless,
                        spiraling downward.
Where will it lead?

Sparks of truth
        providing a way
                out and up
away and around.

Sparks of hope
        opening our eyes,
                showing us a path
                        out of the darkness

 | LISA LEVINE

**Returning to the Table, a *Midrash* poem**

After I had been banished b God
for gossiping about my *gi-oret toshav*
sister-in-law Tzippora,
there came the day I had to return
to the camp and face her.

Who could blame her for hating me?
Indeed, I had spoken ill of her
to the community.
Something had set me off
and I couldn't hold my tongue
even though I knew it was wrong.

For that mistake, I almost paid
with my life.
My skin turned white.
Moses pleaded, *"El Na, R'fana La"*
and God spared me.
I had time to think about
the error of my ways
and how my words hurt the ones I love.

So it's time for me to make my apologies
and return to your table.
Should I bring a gift? an offering?
What can I do to make amends?
should I be honest and tell you
that my jealousy and immaturity kept me
from accepting you as our own?

Your table is always filled to overflowing
with people and tasty dishes
even here in the wilderness.
You set a lovely repast for family
and strangers alike.
After all, you and Moses are the leaders
of this rag-tag lot of stragglers.

All this I thought to myself,
and I tried to think of what I was going to say.

Finally the day came and I squared my shoulders.
I entered your tent and said "Hello."
You responded with a smile and said,
"I'm glad to see you back with us, Miriam.
Please, come and sit with us. Eat."

I should have known that you would
forgive me, without a word, an explanation.
I learned a lot about you that day.
I learned that a forgiving heart
is more precious than gold.
I learned that time, sometimes,
is the only healer,
and that with patience, kindness, and grace,
I can learn to forgive myself.

| LISA LEVINE

**Freedom**

It takes courage
to face life's challenges,
it takes understanding
to accept injustice.
Just as our ancestors
left their oppressors
with faith as their weapon,
so do we
harness our inner warrior
to navigate tumultuous
waters,
moments in our lives,
moments in our history,
adapting, changing,
coping, growing.
We rise
to overcome our demons,
we accept
our inevitabilities,
we conquer
each day with new purpose,
we rejoice
in our endeavors.
And when we fail,
we learn that
our journey is the path leading us
home.

**The Light of You**

As we bring healing to those in need of strength,

    May our spirits be filled with the light of You.

As we bring hope to a broken world.

    May our hearts be softened by the light of You.

As we bring understanding to those who are suffering,

    May our arms be opened by the light of You.

As we bring awareness to hatred,

    May our anger be lessened by the light of You.

As we bring calm for inner peace,

    May our breath be deepened by the light of You.

And may You guide us to those who seek our gifts,

    Leading them gently and lovingly,

        To the light of You. Amen.

LISA LEVINE, is a well known cantor, composer, author, chaplain, poet and recording artist. Her poems and writings are included in *The Women's Torah Commentary, Women of Reform Judaism Covenant Collections, Lombardi Voices, Georgetown Medstar University Hospital Poetry Cafés,* Neshama National Association for Jewish Chaplains newsletters, *Reformed Judiasm* and *jVOICE*. Her book *Yoga Shalom* was featured by the Jewish Book Council. Lisa was ordained though HUC-JIR DFSSM as Cantor and through Aleph Alliance for Jewish Renewal as Rabbinic Pastor. Her liturgical and healing music is widely recorded, published and celebrated. She serves various communities in the mid-Atlantic region as worship ritual artist, cantor, teacher and religious leader. Lisa teaches yoga embodiment, chant and meditation, chaplaincy and music in communities, conferences and congregations around the world. She resides in the Washington D.C. area with her husband Andy Levine and shares her life with her children Emily and Louis. You can learn more at her website: www.cantorlisalevine.com

www.ingramcontent.com/pod-product-compliance
Lightning Source LLC
Chambersburg PA
CBHW042339150426
43195CB00006B/114